# Miniature Horses, Mini Horses and Mini Ponies as pets.

## Care, health, training, playing, costs and where to buy all included.

by

Elliott Lang

# Published by IMB Publishing 2013

# Table of Contents

# Table of Contents

# Table of Contents

# Introduction

Miniature horses make fantastic pets. They are a wonderful
addition to any herd and they work well as companion animals
to larger horses. Miniature horses are such entertaining little
animals, scampering about the place with their cheeky grins and
mischievous look in their eye. They can even be used as
assistance animals for the blind. The most important tool you
can have, when considering any pet, is knowledge and
information is the key to keeping both you and your animal safe
and well. If you've already got one or are thinking about getting
one, this book will give you access to the knowledge and
understanding that will allow you to make an informed choice
about miniature horses in your life.

# Chapter 1) Miniature horses

So you're looking at miniature horses, maybe you're thinking about getting one as a pet or a companion for another animal, perhaps you're just curious. Whatever the reason, this book is a good place to start.

## *1. What exactly is a miniature horse?*

Miniature horses have been bread for as long as we have been domesticating horses, as companion animals for both people and larger horses. They have been selectively bred not only for their size, but also for their temperament. Miniature horses from long lines and old breeds tend to be very sound animals; stable in their behaviour and in their health. Like all horses, they are measured to the withers, which is the ridge between the shoulder blades of the horse. All heights of horses are given to the withers, so when someone says that their horse is 19 inches tall; they mean that the horse is 19 inches plus neck and head. This is because horses do not stand with their heads up straight, and can often have very different neck angles from each other.

Miniature horses can be anything from 14" up to the larger ones at 34" or so. They can weigh as little as 20lbs, although many weigh more than 40bls. There are so many variations and individual oddities among miniature horses that it is difficult to pin down the specific sizes horses need to be in order to be classed as miniatures, as some horses are heavier for their size than others.

They have been selectively bred for size either by humans, or indeed, by nature. There are many instances of early wild horses being much smaller than what we picture in our mind today when we think of a horse. Grass has a very low nutritional value and can be very difficult to digest and metabolise. A lot of energy is taken up in moving about and the larger an animal is the more energy it costs to move. In areas of poor grazing, animals with less 'expensive' bodies, the smaller ones, tend to survive to breed, and thus natural selection, as well as human intervention, has caused a strong gene for 'small' horses in the general horse population.

As they are mostly bred down from regular sized horses, miniature horses are available in all of the colours and patterns that their larger cousins are. While miniature horses are limited in stature, they come in all sorts of shapes. Like their larger counterparts, they can be stocky and sturdy, or fine boned and elegant.

A miniature horse is not the same as a horse with dwarfism. Dwarfism is rare in full-sized horses, but not so rare in miniature horses. Some breeders have bred dwarfism genes into their miniatures in order to take short cuts in the shrinking of these little animals, but this is incredibly detrimental to the physical and mental health of the animals involved.

## 2. Types of miniature horse

Most miniature horses come in all of the colour varieties available in their full sized counterparts. From palomino to piebald and skewbald, there are many colours, patterns and shapes available. There are 2 main types of body shape in miniature horses. The American and Falabella horses tend to have the more refined Arabian look, being sleeker and daintier. Other types of miniature horses err on the chunkier side, having a more cart horse/quarter horse shape to them.

### Falabella

The stunning little Falabella is one of the smallest breeds of horses in the world. Rarely bigger than 32 inches tall, Falabella horses are usually 28 to 34 inches. They are incredibly dainty creatures, with real cob proportions (often looking like a regular horse that is further away than you thought it was). Falabella foals are ridiculously cute and small, born at around a foot tall. Only able to be ridden by small children, Falabella horses are usually shown in-hand. They were originally used to pull carts and are commonly still driven. They make great pets because of their good temperament and small size. There is a formal breed registry for Falabella horses and they have their own association of breeders (Falabella Horse Breeders Association). Falabella miniature horses are much easier to get hold of in the US than the UK, as they originated in Argentina. These horses are considered rare, although there are lots of miniature horses with Falabella genes. True Falabella horses will have very little in the way of dwarfism in their family history, as Falabella breeders were going for the dainty, full size horse proportions, rather than small and cute.

**American miniature horse**

The American Miniature Horse is an absolutely lovely animal with many good qualities. They tend to look more like shrunken racehorses than ponies or other miniatures tend to. They are fine boned and elegant with strong personalities and generally good tempers, although they can be a little more skittish than Shetland, Welsh or Falabella minis.

Like Falabella horses, they are available in a wide range of colours and patterns, but unlike the Falabella, the American is relatively easy to get hold of in the UK as well as the US, with much larger numbers having been bred and sold, and they are more readily available and less expensive to purchase (although the lifetime costs are the same). If you can get an American with good, strong bloodlines and no family history of dwarfism then they make good, healthy pets. You have to be careful if you chose an American Miniature Horse as there are some, I stress not many, breeders who actively breed dwarfism genes into their stock to shrink their animals down.

## Shetland pony

They have small heads, thick shoulders and good, strong legs. Shetland ponies are one of the most popular breeds of miniature horses. While some believe that ponies cannot be true miniature horses, if ponies and horses can breed with no ill consequences they must be the same species, so a little pony must be a little horse. As the name suggests, the Shetland pony is a pony from the Shetland Isles (off the coast of Scotland). Shetlands are among the hardiest of miniature horses, being bred for the harsh landscape and heavy work load associated with the Isles they lived on and later the collieries they worked in during the British industrial revolution. They tend to be stocky about the legs and long in the body, sometimes appearing as though they have been cut short at the knee, giving them a comical look when they stand in muddy fields or run along beside other animals.

They can be quite elegant though, as their breeding has been much less restrictive than that of New World miniatures, and their bloodline will often have some Arab or thoroughbred in there somewhere. They are often used for racing and a quick internet search will give you hundreds of examples of the little guys tearing round the track at lightening speeds, usually with children riding them. Due to their slightly heavier build, they are able to carry more weight comfortably than their fine boned cousins.

As with the other types mentioned, Shetland ponies come in a range of colours and shapes, from red to black and white spotted like a Dalmatian and anything in between. Because of their history as working animals, there is very little in the way of dwarfism in Shetland ponies, despite their chunky good looks.

**Welsh pony/cob**

Although these are larger than the other breeds, they are still classed as miniatures as they can be quite small. There is evidence that these horses have been around, in some form, for over 3,000 years. These horses have a high level of stamina and are great for driving. Welsh ponies and Welsh cobs are often grouped together. Being small, colliery animals from Wales it is easy to see why. There are 4 categories of Welsh horses, called sections A, B, C and D.

The Welsh Mountain Pony, (section A) has a small head, large eyes, a high tail and will often show a slightly dished face. This is because of the strong influence of the Arabian horse in it's past. A section A cannot be taller than 50 inches in the US or 48 inches in the UK.

Welsh Riding Ponies, (section B) are much larger, not being taller than 54 inches, though they can be classed as miniatures by some associations. They are daintier than the section A horses and more closely resemble the larger Thoroughbreds and Hackneys in their history. These are usually used as riding horses for children and they jump really well.

The Welsh Cob type Pony (section C) is an animal that much more closely resembles the cob than the pony. Being up to 54 inches tall, the Cob Type is quite large for a mini and is very well muscled.

Welsh Cobs, (section D) are not miniature, they are much too tall to be described as miniature, although they are lovely animals.

**Gypsy Vanner**

While not always a miniature horse, the Gypsy Vanner has an excellent temperament. Ranging from 12 to 16 hands (48 to 64 inches) tall, the gypsy cob originated in Great Britain and the British isles, and was bread by the gypsy people, mainly for their gentle nature, secondly for health, and thirdly for their stunning looks. They really are beautiful, with sturdy bodies and huge amounts of feathering at the leg with lovely colour patterns, being mostly piebald and skewbald. Still used in gypsy communities for driving, occasionally still for drawing caravans, and for children to ride, the Gypsy Vanner is a good, reliable, working horse. There are about 2,200 registered in the US and 2,000 registered in the UK, though there are many crosses.

The Gypsy Vanner is an incredibly hardy animal; less prone to many of the illnesses and injuries that trouble horses in general. These horses are so gentle and aware of where people are that they make fantastic first horses, to the point where you will often find them with children crawling about on or around them. Their heavyset bone structure means that they are less likely to be skittish or easily spooked and their gentle nature makes them great around children and smaller animals.

**Dartmoor ponies**

Dartmoor ponies are generally caught as foals from feral populations, although many are now bred in captivity. Because of their feral ancestry, Dartmoor ponies can be a little unpredictable in their general size and temperament, although not significantly more than other miniature horses. They make excellent pets and first rider horses for children, but they cannot be ridden until they are about 4 and most Dartmoors bought at a market will be under a year old.

Because they are often born in the wild, with no mother's medical history, Dartmoor ponies will need a lot of observation and care. Daily handling will be required to get the animals used to people. The main advantage of a feral caught horse is the evolutionary breeding – breeding in the wild is risky, and only the healthiest mothers survive, meaning that only the foals with the best chance of survival will make it. Feral caught horses tend to be much more robust and less prone to congenital illness, as in wild populations illness means death. The harsh reality of life in the wild makes these animals far stronger. They will also often have a wider gene pool.

**Crossbreeds**

If you can get hold of a crossbreed then you're in luck. If you don't intend to show as a specific breed or breed to show as a specific breed, then you should really be on the look out for crossbreeds. Crossbreeds have the best temperaments, the least health complications and the smallest price tag. Horses, like dogs, have been bred to within an inch of the gene pool, becoming a gene puddle. A little outside influence can do the long-term health of the genes a power of good. As long as neither parent has a dwarfism in their recent history, crossbreeds are almost always healthier and live longer than pure breeds. This goes for cats, dogs, and sheep. Whatever the animal, a wider gene pool makes for healthier, more stable animals.

A Falabella of an American crossed with a Shetland or a Welsh would give the best results, as there is less likelihood of what exotics breeders call back contamination, where you go back in the family tree and find a loop. The reason for this is very simple; the Atlantic Ocean. This huge expanse of water has meant there has been little contact between the Shetland and Welsh and the Falabella and the American. Any domestically bred horse will produce healthier offspring with a wild/feral cross. Domestic mares that have been bred to feral caught stallions produce very hardy young. Whatever the cross, a crossbred miniature horse will make a much healthier, happier, more stable animal and can be much better as pets.

**The problem with dwarf miniature horses**

It may seem that I'm being awfully harsh on dwarf horses. The truth is they can make good pets if you have massive financial resources or are married to/are a vet, but the intentional breeding in of dwarf genes to shrink down miniature horses causes all sorts of trouble.

Cute as this may seem, dwarfism can cause all sorts of physical, mental and emotional problems, often resulting in animals who are unsound or whose veterinary bills are so high as to render it best to have the animal euthanized.

Their legs often won't form properly, because of a problem converting cartilage into bone, and will need complicated, painful and, often, ongoing surgery. Because of the problems with cartilage, they can have collapses in all sorts of places, including the pharynx, (wind pipe), leaving them in need of a permanent tracheotomy and long-term care to keep infection out of the open hole to their repertory system. Their teeth will often grow to be too big for their mouths and will need to be removed. Dwarf horses are far more likely to be born with an undershot jaw, making eating, breathing and communicating difficult and even painful. The angle of the nose can result in respiratory problems from inhaling rain. The bulging eyes are far more prone to injury from branches and other animals.

Worse are the babies who don't get to be pets. Because of the health complications involved with some forms of dwarfism and inbreeding the dwarfism genes, many dwarf miniature horses do not survive long enough. They can have abnormalities with the heart, lungs and diaphragm, being too big or too small to support the animal. They can be born with serious curvature of the spine. Although these animals with this particular problem will often not survive long after birth and don't end up as people's pets, there is a cruelty in knowingly putting a mare through that risk that people who genuinely care about horses find intolerable.

# Chapter 2) Miniature horses in the wild

A lot of common horse behaviours and quirks can be accounted for by looking at their situation in the wild. This is the same with many animals now domesticated and is put down to a 'genetic memory', or wild instincts that have been retained but no longer necessary for survival. While there is still a lot of argument about when horses were first domesticated, and while it could very well be as long as 6,000 years ago, we have to take into account that geologically, that's not a very long time. Because of this, and because they are already pretty well adapted to human needs, horses display a lot of behaviours that can be traced back to wild survival instincts and can be recognised in prey herds, such as deer, zebra and sheep.

In the wild, most horses tend to live in herds for safety. They live in large, permanent family groups, with the lead mare being in charge. The lead mare will be a mature mare who has proven her dominance over the others, though will generally not be the oldest or the strongest. She will chose when and where the herd moves, drink first from the water holes and ponds and generally be the boss.

The dominant stallion will protect the herd from predators and strange males. A single stallion would be responsible for 'covering' up to 20 females. There may be other males in the herd, but they will be submissive to the dominant male and while they will still defend the herd, they are not responsible for the safety of it in the same way. There will often be several stallions in a herd and they will live quietly and happily together with no problems of dominance or aggression.

Domesticated stallions are often kept apart as they are seen as aggressive towards one another, although this is usually because there has been no opportunity for them to have come into contact and break the tension. Tension between stallions, caused by never establishing who is strongest, can make them very unpredictable around each other and if this builds up they can do each other serious damage. Horses are easily worried by things they don't know, and if an intact male has never encountered another intact male they can be very dangerous. When 2 adult males do meet in the wild, the conflict is often short lived, and usually doesn't result in either animal being badly hurt, as any injury increases the probability of being caught by large predators. Neither animal is likely to take the risk of being hurt themselves in order to hurt the other. The conflict usually involves a lot of posturing and showing off of how big and strong they are, coupled with a lot of eye rolling and noise. These meetings are generally all show and no substance. This means that the animals involved are still strong and able to defend themselves from any predators, should the need arise.

Horses are prey animals. This explains a lot of their behaviour, and you can usually tell by looking at a horse (as with most prey animals) if they will be flighty or calm. Because in the wild anything they don't know could well be trying to eat them, horses can be quite liable to skittish behaviours. Animals with a finer, more elegant looking bone structure are more likely to be damaged in an attack than those with bigger bones.

Chunkier horses tend to be calmer, as they would sustain less damage in an attack and could generally defend themselves better. Even among smaller horses, the less dainty ones tend to be calmer and less likely to be startled easily.

In the wild, horses eat little and often, as they have to digest lots of plant cellulose, which is a tricky process. They will eat a mixture of whatever grazing they can find, which will usually include mainly grass, some wild flowers and grass seeds. The grass they live on tends to be of relatively poor quality, as they are hoofed animals and so survive best in dryer conditions. Because of their comparatively arid surroundings, the grass they live on will be of the hardy, drier variety, such as you'd find on the edge of deserts or near beaches. In captivity, they usually have access to much better quality pasture, and this can cause all sorts of problems.

In the wild, horses tend to be nomadic and migratory, following the seasons and the better pasture, and avoiding drought where it occurs. Because of their sheer size and the relatively low/ difficult to access nutritional grass, especially the wild, dry grasses they tend to have access to, wild horses can cover huge expanses of land and will often travel for many miles at a time. Where their ability to roam has been limited or restricted in any way or the quality of grazing is poor, horses have tended to be smaller and better adapted to using less food, as animals with smaller bodies need less food and will survive to breeding age much better.

There is this wonderful, romantic notion people tend to hold about wild horses. The fact is, though, that most of what we think of as 'wild' horse populations are actually feral groups, as there are very few truly wild horses with no domesticated ancestors. We usually use the word 'wild' to mean free roaming feral horses, like the American Mustangs, the British Moor pony or the Australian Brumby. The properly wild horses are all but extinct, with the Tarpan, or Eurasian Wild Horse being completely extinct and the Przewalski, or Mongolian Wild Horse being on the endangered species list.

British Moor ponies of Dartmore, the Black Forrest and other areas are dying out too. This is because of the difficulty in proving who is responsible for them. Unlike in America and Australia, the harsh winters mean that without shelter and extra food, the British Moor Pony cannot survive. They will often not be fed or protected over the winter, as the landowners will claim that the animals are the responsibility of neighbours, other owners or even the RSPCA.

However, the landowners will often catch and sell the foals of these wild animals. Because landowners can potentially make a profit from these animals on their land, they have a responsibility for their welfare. Even if there was no profit involved, UK law states very clearly that domestic animals are the responsibility of the keeper. The keeper is defined as the person in possession of the animal or its environment. Horses are classed as domesticated, agricultural animals.

Whilst most miniature horses have been bred down from a larger horse, there are minis in the wild. In places where food and grazing is scarce, smaller animals are more likely to survive to breed, as they can survive on less food.

On the Shetland Isles (off the cost of Scotland), for example, smaller horses have been favoured since the Bronze Age. They are sturdy, hardy and quite even-tempered. They can be as little as 19" high.

# Chapter 3) Miniature horses as pets

Miniature horses make excellent pets, and have done for an incredibly long time.

## 1. History and original source of pet miniature horses

Miniature horses have been around for quite a long time, and have been domesticated for as long other horses. Specific breeds of miniature horses have been artificially created by humans for different purposes, although temperament has, historically, been high up on the list of attributes.

Miniature horses have been used as first horses for children, and to pull carriages and hacks for almost as long as horses have been kept domestically. They have a rich and important history with humans, and have contributed hugely to human development, not least the industrial revolution.

With the invention of steam power came a greater demand for coal than the world had ever seen, and with that increase in demand, came the rise if the pit pony. Pit ponies were small, hardy, and horrifically ill-treated.

Pit ponies were often never brought out into the daylight, so that no time would be wasted getting their eyes accumulated to light and dark. They worked underground their entire lives, and when they were no longer fit to work, they would be brought out into the blinding light and left to die. This horrendous legacy has meant that most small horses are very strong for their size and have incredibly high stamina.

## 2. Is this the pet for you? Pros and cons of miniature horses

Miniature horses are excellent animals to have around and make such good pets. They are great with people and other animals. There are lots of excellent reasons to keep miniature horses as pets.

### Herd

Horses need to live in a herd, but the herd doesn't need to be a traditional herd of horses. They can live in any herd type, from one or 2 other horses around or a whole field of them to a couple of goats or sheep.

### House

Miniature horses make great pets for the house-proud. They don't live in the house, so there isn't really any chance of them soiling your furniture or carpets. They are also less likely to shed fur on your clothing, reducing mess. They are also great at keeping large lawns down.

## Allergies

Miniature horses make great cuddly pets for those who want to have a furry pet to stroke and make fuss of and spend time with but who have asthma or other allergies. You are far less likely to be allergic to horses than you are to cats or dogs.

## Cost

They are small enough to be considered pets rather than livestock. Large horses can be a real drain financially and miniature horses will usually cost a lot less to keep than a large horse, although this will be dependant on any medical conditions.

There are so many positive reasons to keep miniature horses. They are such lovely, companionable animals that can add to your life in so many ways. But there are also many difficulties that you should take into consideration. You need to be able to look after them properly and there are some very important questions that you need to ask yourself before you go any further:

## Can you afford it?

They can be very costly, not just in the initial outlay on the animal itself but the feeding and housing requirements also need to be taken into consideration. As well as this, you may need to lay out for medical expenses, (vet bills, medicine and travel to and from the vets if they are not close)

**Can you cope with a grumpy/huffy miniature horse and keep up the daily handing and fussing to get them back to their sweet old self?**

Being able to get a huffy, stressed or shy miniature horse can be vital to keeping them with you and out of a shelter or worse. Horses that become difficult to handle because of a minor incident putting the owners off, meaning they spend less time with their pet, are increasingly a problem for animal charities, and animals with behavioural problems often have to be put down.

**Will you be available to clean the housing out often enough?**

You need to clean them out completely and change all of their bedding and litter every week, including making sure their toys are clean. You'll also need to do a spot clean every day, taking out any obvious soiling and wet bedding.

**Do you have enough space for a miniature horse?**

They need a large space to move about in. Just because they are miniature does not mean that they can be kept in a small yard. They need access to grazing, as well as a space they can be kept away from ground that is too lush. They also need access to somewhere indoors where they can be out of the weather, such as a shed, barn or even a stable. If you have other horses, a miniature horse will fit in around them, but if not, their space requirements could be larger than you anticipated.

**What would you do if they bit you?**

Could you cope with the idea that your lovely cute baby has hurt you on purpose? While the bite may not be vindictive, it can really hurt your feelings when something you have nurtured and loved breaks the trust and snaps at you. While it is unlikely, all animals can bite, and a horse bite can be quite nasty. If this happens, you need to be able to pull yourself together and get on with making your horse safe again. This can only happen if you remain calm and collected. Being in control of yourself can be hard if your pet distresses you.

**Can you meet their dietary requirements?**

They need grain, hay and grass on a daily basis. If your miniature horse develops laminitis, you will need to restrict their access to pasture and provide more hay.

**Can you make a 25-35 year commitment to love and care for your miniature horse?**

Even if you buy your miniature horse older, you could well be in for a long commitment. The oldest recorded miniature horse lived to be 50-years-old. Many people will sell a horse after a few years and the horse will still be healthy and happy, but will you be able to make that decision? What if you can't find a buyer for an older horse?

## 3. Costs

Aside from the initial cost of buying your miniature horse, there are a lot of other things you'll need to take into consideration. Keeping a horse can cost well over $1600 or £1000 a year, not to mention any emergencies or unexpected expenses.

**Land**

If you've already got horses or similar animals, the cost of land won't be an issue. The same applies if you've got a lot of space already that you plan to keep your miniature horse in. However, if you plan on buying or renting land for your new addition, this can be a large initial outlay or a long-term, ongoing cost. You could end up needing to rent space for your miniature horse for over 20 years. As most people who keep miniature horses do so to keep them as companions to other animals, this isn't something they need to worry about, but if you are going to have a pet miniature horse and don't have existing space, you'll need to either buy or rent somewhere with stabling.

**Show fees**

Many horse owners choose to show their animals, and while this is an optional extra, it can be expensive, with fees ranging from £7 /$10 to £70 /$100.

**Food**

As miniature horses are more prone to laminitis, they cannot just

27

live on sweet, fresh grass. They will need taking off of the grass and restricting to hay at least some of the time. They will also need an allowance of grain and oats.

**Insurance and vet fees**

Insurance or vet fees can be quite high. They need the hoofs trimming regularly, they need worming every 8 weeks and they need vaccinating against various illnesses.

**Accessories**

You might not need all the gubbins that you would have for a standard sized horse, such as saddles, stirrups, boots and helmets, but you will need a bridle, and these are not much cheaper than a full sized bridle, as the same amount of work goes into them.

Here is an overall summary of the costs:

Grass keep: £450/ $800
Feed, hay, etc: £100/ $160
Vet's fees (inc. teeth and vaccinations): £80/ $130
Insurance: £170/ $220
Farrier: £240/ $380
Worming: £60/ $100
TOTAL ANNUAL COST: £1100/ £1790

PLUS APPROX ONE-OFF COSTS:
Passport: £10/ $
Training (when your miniature horse is old enough): £500/ $

Tack / Equipment: £500/ $
TOTAL ONE OFF COSTS £1010/ $

## *4. Other animals*

Miniature horses are the perfect companion animals for all sorts of creatures. If introduced to lots of animals at an early age, there are no animals that would be a problem, although un-gelded males may be picked on by a larger, intact male, herd animals, and large dogs and should never be left alone with any prey animal. No matter how well trained, if a dog takes down a horse, it is instinct, not malice, that has causes the problem.

They get on particularly well with goats, donkeys and sheep. There is a very cute video on youtube of a miniature stallion 'herding' his harem of female goats in the snow.

Larger, show or race quality horses are expensive to keep, and most are kept away from other large horses to avoid injury or stress, but they can become lonely and very uneasy, and sometimes unwell, if they are left alone. Horses are herd animals and should not be kept completely isolated, as this can cause stress, behavioural problems and illness. Miniature horses make the ideal companion for such animals, being able to share their space and, to an extent, their food, worming medicine and supplements.

## 5. Health benefits of miniature horses

There have been ideas for years that pets are good for your health. Stroking a cat or dog has a soothing affect and the responsibility of pet ownership has a generally stabilizing effect on mood and behavior. Studies have shown that owning a pet can increase the levels of endorphins in the brain and can increase physical health, improve sleep patterns and stave off illness. Pets can reduce the symptoms of depression. The soothing, repetitive action of stroking a pet has been proven to lower blood pressure.

**How do Miniature horses fit in with this?**

Because of the closeness of the bond between a miniature horse and their owner, the love and affection shown can seriously improve one's mood.

If you find yourself becoming isolated, pets, especially less common ones, are really good icebreakers. By joining an owners' forum and going to meetings and shows you can find that you have a network of friends across the world.

Pets can really push you to social interaction in ways that you are not being negatively judged. The depth of the bond between a miniature horse and it's people mean that they make great companion animals.

It's strange, but even when you struggle to take care of yourself emotionally, having a dependant who relies on you to get out of bed and feed and cuddle "can help give you a sense of your own value and importance" according to Dr Ian Cook, director of Depression Research (UCLA).

The uncomplicated nature of the bond between a miniature horse and their owner can be a great antidote to complex family and social relationships.

Having a routine with your miniature horse can add structure to your day and this is a fantastic way to keep your mental health on track.

# Chapter 4) Caring for your Miniature horse

## *1. Housing requirements*

Miniature horses have very specific enclosure requirements, which are similar, though not identical, to other hoofed animals, such as other horses and goats.

Some owners allow their miniature horses complete free reign over their paddock, bringing them in only at night or in poor weather. This is not advisable, however, because of their tendency to contract laminitis, a painful condition caused by too much lush pasture. Miniature horses are more prone to this than full sized horses, and so cannot be allowed the same freedom to roam as perhaps their larger companions.

They can live in adapted wooden Wendy houses or sheds or they can live in full sized stables with larger horses. Their housing needs to be well ventilated but it must keep the wind out. The housing should be roomy enough for the horse to move about, lie down and roll comfortably. The British Horse Society suggests the recommended minimum dimensions for ponies should be 3.0m x 3.0m and 3.0m x 3.6m for larger ponies.

Your horse will also need a field shelter to protect them from the weather when they're out in the pasture. They need protection from any bad weather, but also from high heat. A small pony will only require a 3.0x 3.6m shelter, whereas a larger horse would ideally require a 4.5m x 3.6m shelter as a minimum size to ensure a comfortable, safe environment.

You need to make sure that wherever your miniature horse lives, they can reach everything and that any food, water and toys are at miniature height. If there are larger horses in the stables, that should be fine, but you have to make sure that your mini horse can reach everything.

It may seem a nice idea to have your miniature horse sleep in your house with you. This is very bad for your horse. They belong outdoors in the daytime and in their own house at night. Even assistance horses, which spend the majority of their day indoors one way or another, need to be outside (ish) at night.

**Space and enclosure types:**

The difference in space requirements between miniature horses and standard horses is huge. Many are kept in large gardens, with assistance animals living in.

**Should you have only one or a whole herd?**

Because of the nature of these diminutive little loves, you

shouldn't be looking at getting more than one at a time. If you already have other farm type animals, a miniature horse will assimilate them into their herd. Un-gelded male horses can be quite aggressive to one another, and this should also be considered when thinking about companion animals. The amount of time and effort involved in keeping these animals is such that you really need to think carefully about keeping more of them.

While they are herd animals, they don't need their herd to be of the same species. If they are going to be kept at communal stables or in a farm/small holding environment then you really don't need more than one of them. If you don't have any other animals and the miniature horse won't be kept with other peoples animals, then you might consider getting a couple of them, or a donkey/sheep/goat to live with them.

## 2. Feeding and treats

The nutritional needs of miniature horses are not very difficult to meet if you know what to look for. You should try to keep their diet as natural as possible. In the wild, horses evolved to eat wild grasses, seeds and windfall fruit.

They need a lot of hay and grass, with additional grain feed depending on the quality of the grazing, with supplements of salt and other minerals, as well as fruit/vegetable treats.

Apple, carrots, horse nuts and sweeds make great treats and aren't too bad for your horses teeth. Some owners give sugar free mints. Others allow sugary sweets, like palmer violets etc, but this is something you need to think about for the long-term health of your miniature horse, as they can develop diabetes and other problems relating to sugar.

You also need to provide fresh drinking water. There should always be more water available than the horse might need. Water should be clean and have no algae or other contaminants.

### *Tree, shrub and plant material*

Horses like to strip bark and nibble at trees and shrubs. Any plant material within reach of your miniature horse should be edible and expendable; if your horse can reach it, they'll probably eat it. Having the odd branch to chew on won't do your horse any harm and will be good for their teeth, providing abrasive 'brushing' and wearing them.

Horses all like a good scratch, and being able to have a good ole rub against a branch is a great way for them to give themselves a little scratch. Be careful that there are no very sharp points on anything that can hurt your horse though.

Just be very aware not to have any plants that you're particularly fond of within reach of your miniature horse; they will get nibbled.

## 3. Useful websites for buying housing, food and treats

### Housing
UK www.ebay.co.uk

USA www.ebay.com

**Toys and tack**

UK
www.likit.co.uk
www.equineclothing.co.uk
www.miniponytack.com

USA
www.forminisonly.com
www.minitack.com
www.equi-spirit-toys.com
www.theminiaturehorseshop.com

# Chapter 5) Settling in your horse

## *1. Bonding*

You need to spend a lot of time bonding with your horse. With miniature horses, because of their size, the most common way to train them is with something called natural horsemanship. This is an idea that horses should at no point be in pain or fear of pain at any point. Practitioners describe this as being radical departure from "traditional" techniques, which are often portrayed as being based on the use of unnecessary force.

Horses respond to tones of voice. Always use a soft, soothing tone when you are near your horse. It will relax him/her. You need to make sure that your voice doesn't upset your horse.

Be careful not to shout or scream when you are around your horse as this can make him stressed and he may panic and lash out. If a horse is spooked, even a small horse, they could be dangerous. If you spook them, it is not their fault if they misbehave, it is yours.

You should spend time around your horse when you are calm and relaxed to make sure your horse recognises you as being safe. Your horse needs to be able to trust you. You should make sure your horse knows that you will never let them down. If he has an itch, scratch it for him. Never do big, sudden movements that could spook them.

You should groom your miniature horse as much as possible,

stroking them, being around them, getting them used to the idea that you are a source of possible comfort. Express your feelings for your horse in a way that he will understand. You can rub their shoulder or pinch with the *pads* of your fingers (not the nail) on the crest of his mane, this imitates the way horses groom each other, and he will understand what you are trying to say, and will return your affection.

Don't pull away if the horse tries to sniff or nibble on you. He is simply returning your affection, and will be confused if you don't accept it. Hold your hand out and let him smell you; if you let your horse get used to your scent, it will also help you to bond.

## 2. *Preparing for your miniature horse*

You need to get a lot of things ready before you bring your miniature horse home. You'll need to be prepared, and there are a few things you should have sorted out.

### Land and stabling

You need to have the land where your horse will live checked out and safe. You should know in advance that your miniature horse will be safe and have room to move about.

### Other animals

You shouldn't bring a horse of any size to live anywhere where they will be alone. You should have other animals about to help them settle in. As herd creatures, they are much more comfortable around other herd animals. One of the most important things, after food and shelter, is companionship and your miniature horse's life with you will be off to a great start if they feel happy and comfortable, and having other animals there from the offset will make this much more likely.

## 3. Shopping list

Ivermectin
Grass keep
Feed, hay,
Antiseptic
Passport
Wormer
Toys
Styptic
Vaccines
Animalintex Poultice
Antiseptic
Electrolyte compound

**Logbook**

For many horse owners a logbook may be a little OTT in the way of being organised, but for many others, it can be a lifesaver. By keeping accurate records that can be accessed and understood by anyone who might need information about your miniature horse's habits, behaviour, feeding and medications, you will be keeping your horse safe, even if you are not the only one to be looking after them. It can mean your vet may be able to pinpoint the sources or beginning of any illnesses. This will also be useful if you come to sell your miniature horse later on.

The back pages should be a calendar, with dates not days, where you can mark on the worming, farrier and vaccine dates. If you do these things to a strict routine, then there will be far less problems of overlap or missing them out. This is also very useful if there are two or more people involved in the care of the animal. Keeping a record of any medical intervention is very handy too, and knowing when exactly they are administered can help to identify bad interactions.

The front pages should contain a list of useful phone numbers (vet, farrier, insurance details), any regular medications the animal is taking and their description/passport information. This can be very useful in case there are any problems when someone else is watching your horse, for example when you are on holiday.

Internal pages should be a week or 2 per page with a line about each visit to the horse. You should record feed given, any changes in the movement/gait of the horse, interactions with other animals etc. You should also make a record of any time your miniature horse is in transit and how they react to this. If they are ever weighed or measured, you should write this down. If they don't seem to have been eating or drinking, this should also be noted.

# Chapter 6) Natural Horsemanship

Natural horsemanship is the proper name for horse whispering. This is now the accepted way to train little horses, and you don't need to be a professional horse trainer, you just need to spend time with your horse and learn how to understand them.

In 1981, lifelong horseman, rodeo rider, horse trainer, cowboy and teacher Pat Parelli founded the Parelli Program, a program of horse training that involved not fear or dominance. He was joined by his wife, Linda Parelli, in 1993. The Parelli Program focuses on teaching the human rather than training the horse.

Early on, Pat realized that horses already had all the skills they needed to thrive in their world; they would have been extinct centuries ago otherwise! He discovered that understanding the psychology, personality and nature of horses could become the basis for a deep, seamless and reciprocally beneficial human-horse relationship.

Pat named his new relationship-based approach "Natural Horsemanship", and it is commonly known as horse whispering, which is now recognized worldwide as an innovative and effective method of natural, gentle horse training. To get your horse to do what you want without any pain or fear is the aim of this method, and your horse will be much less likely to revert to pre-training behaviour and if they are never given cause to fear humans, they will make much better pets, and be much calmer and easier to handle in general.

The Parelli approach is not to train horses, but to teach each horse owner to become his or her own horse trainer, and to succeed by building a relationship of trust with each horse. Of course, horsemanship skills are taught in the Parelli program, but the foundation of the method is built on the relationship with the principles of Love, Language and Leadership as guides.

This method teaches that, as a horse owner and trainer, you should be able to:

- Succeed without force so that your horse should only ever see you in a positive light. It is about persuasion and trust.

- Develop a partnership without dominance, where there is no one in charge. The relationship between you and your horse will be a genuine partnership.

- Work with your horse without fear. Neither horse nor owner should be in fear at any point. This is also very useful if you are working with a small horse you are fond of. You'll never have to be horrid to your little lovely.

*"People realize this is what they've been looking for in all their relationships," comments Pat Parelli. "It's balanced with love, language and leadership in equal doses. The program and the horse give them a living model so they can practice and become fluent in their abilities in all relationships, not just horse relationships."*

*"It's about more than just the horse," echoes Linda. "It really dips into the personal development side of things. You learn about yourself, you learn about communication, about leadership, about truthfulness, about consequence and*

*responsibility. You learn about love and imagination. The horse becomes the animal that tells you the truth about yourself in all these categories."*

Horse owners who follow the Parelli program have found that not only does the program enable them to become a gifted horse trainer, and not only do they achieve exciting horsemanship successes, but they come away with the lasting gift of an enhanced relationship and communication with their horse. Perhaps the greatest gift of all, however, is that they discover enhanced relationships and communication with everyone in their lives.

Pat and Linda's individual life stories are enlightening and extraordinary, and their love of and dedication to horses is palpable, but it is their common vision and mission for Parelli Natural Horsemanship that truly inspires. So much more than horse trainers, Pat and Linda have dedicated their lives and Parelli International to *making the world a better place for horses and humans.*

To build a healthy relationship between you and your horse, you must communicate with the horse in a way he or she will understand. Horses are herd animals, and when you communicate with them, you become the horse's herd. He will depend on you, let you ride him, and be your best friend. Your horse will treat you like another horse, and you will ride and live in harmony. Be sure to talk to him/her a lot when you are with them. They get used to the sound of your voice and recognize it when you come and go.

Be aware that natural horsemanship puts the horse in charge, but not in a dangerous way.

Understand that horses are flight animals because in the wild they are prey animals. Knowing this will help you encourage your horse when it spooks.

# Chapter 7) Health

There are some important things you can do for your horse's long-term health.

Horses need to be vaccinated against flu and rhino in spring and autumn (fall); encephalomyelitis (EEE, WEE) in the spring and strep (strangles) in the fall. They also need a tetanus jab every year and a rabies jab every couple of years; this is where your logbook will come in really handy to keep a record of who's had what and when, especially if you have horses bought at different times. A good equine vet will advise you on the types and amounts of vaccine that can be used for miniature horses, as the dosage needs to be adjusted to accommodate their diminutive size.

Get their hoofs trimmed and looked at every 8 weeks. Hoof pain and problems in horses are a serious and often under valued problem. A horse of any size with bad feet will be in horrific pain, as the relative pressure of the whole horse on such little feet is huge! People sometimes try to cut corners by having the feet looked at less often. This can cause much bigger, long-term expense. If problems with the hoof aren't noticed soon enough, the hoof and the bone can become separated. The hoof is there to protect the blood vessels in the foot and the bone. If blood or bone infections occur, this can be terminal. Hooves left to grow uncontrolled can cause the animal to walk strangely, and can deform and even break the bones in the leg.

Keep your land clear of ragwort. If you have horses already, you will know the terrible dangers caused by this innocuous looking weed. It has lots of cheerful yellow flowers all clustered together and a sort of torn look to its leaves. It can kill horses. It causes permanent liver damage and has an accumulative effect. Smaller horses can tolerate even lower doses than standard horses, and there is no way of knowing if your animal has been exposed to ragwort in the past. A little nibble on the way to a different paddock, a bit or two in a neighbouring field, it all adds up. And what it adds up to as a slow, painful and untreatable death.

The horse will be in a lot of pain as the liver shuts down and the body begins to give up. The horse becomes lacklustre and tired. They experience horrific stomach pains. They stop being able to eat and the weight loss is severe and rapid. Breathing becomes difficult as the lungs shut down. Their balance goes and the horse will appear drunk. The skin becomes painful. The horse will go blind. If a vet believes a horse has ragwort poisoning, they will suggest euthanasia. This is the only kind thing to do in this case.

In the UK, if your fields are invaded by ragwort from a neighbouring field, you can apply for an order for them to be removed as an'injurious weed', as provided for in the Weeds Act of 1959. It isn't law for ragwort to be controlled automatically, but you can apply for an order of notice for them to be removed. While the law here is quite clear, if you aren't confident about it, speak to DEFRA, they are your friend in this and can really get stuff done.

## 1. Common health conditions

Many of the common health problems you will encounter as a horse owner can be either prevented or easily treated with good management and observation. That said, if you are ever in any sort of doubt about anything unusual going on with your animal, you should seek veterinary advice.

### Lice, fleas, mites and parasites

Miniature horses do not seem to get flees, but they can get mites, lice and worms. A heavy parasite burden can cause serious anaemia and with miniature horses this can be fatal much quicker than with larger animals. Even if your miniature horse survives a serious parasite burden, they could be left with some pretty horrific health problems as a result of organ damage. This is easily avoided, however, with the correct, regular preventative treatment and observation.

Mites, lice, ticks and other external parasites can be kept in check with regular grooming.

Miniature horses need worming every 8 weeks. You can do this yourself with an oral de-wormer such as Ivermectin. If your horse is very young or stressed you should use a milder wormer or a daily wormer.

### Obesity

Miniature horses are far more prone to over-eating than larger horses, and because of their stature, the relative weight gain is greater. Because of the smaller size of their gut, miniature horses are only able to process small amounts of food at a time and so should be fed often, but only small amounts. Miniature horses are less likely to get the exercise and restriction of access to pasture. Owners of larger horses can have real emotional niggles about feeding their minis so much less than everyone else. If your miniature horse does become overweight, you need to seek veterinary advice before restricting the diet as there could be an underlying cause (other than gluttony).

**Diarrhoea**

This can be caused by a number of things including infections in the upper or lower gut and eating inappropriate foods or even a change in diet. Diarrhoea, whatever the underlying cause, can be fatal and any horse with diarrhoea should be given plenty of water with electrolytes. It causes rapid dehydration and you should seek veterinary advice as soon as you notice any faeces that are loose or watery.

If your horse has diarrhoea, you need to keep their bedding scrupulously clean and be very aware of hygiene, as if an infection has caused the problem, the animal could accidentally re-infect itself.

Affected animals should be kept away from other animals to avoid further contamination. Your emergency kit should contain ProBalance or some probiotic and, oddly enough, liquorice. The probiotic should help to restore the lost gut flora and the liquorice should reduce digestive inflammation. You still need to see your vet about underlying causes.

**Founder or Laminitis**

More common in horses with access to lots of lush pasture and sweet grass, Founder or Laminitis is a serious and debilitating illness that can reoccur even after it has been treated and subsided. It is a common and very painful condition affecting the feet. Laminitis is where the laminae, the tissue that connects the bone to the hoof, become inflamed. In severe cases, the hoof can become detached from the laminae. Then the bone, which now has no support, can twist around and even work it's way through the sole of the foot.

The best way to describe laminitis to someone with no hoofs, so people, is as if you were to have your fingernails and toenails pushed up out of the nail bed, but the nail bed itself, and then have the bones of your digits push through the flesh. Gruesome as that may sound, it is important that you understand the potential pain involved. Symptoms of advanced laminitis are obvious- the horse will move differently and will be in a huge amount of pain.

Usually, however, if you have a good, regular farrier or if you regularly check the animal's feet to trim the hoof yourself, laminitis can be caught in the early stages, before it becomes painful. If your horse has laminitis, seek veterinary advice, as treatment may include surgery, and will probably include some antibiotic and anti-inflammatory medications.

**Colic**

Colic is an abdominal pain that can be very uncomfortable and can be caused by many different underlying problems.

The symptoms of colic are: trying to look at it's tummy, scratching at the ground, biting their tummy, stretching and moving like they need to pee, restlessness. These are all symptoms that your miniature horse has mild colic. If you notice it at this point you should move to relieve the discomfort, if symptoms persist or reoccur regularly, you should contact your vet. Keep note of any instances of mild colic in your logbook. Sweating, breathing fast/hyper ventilating, lying down on their back, redness of the gums and/or eyes, rapid pulse, rolling on the floor and sitting like a dog, violence and manic rolling are all symptoms of serious colic, and you should seek veterinary advice as soon as possible.

Colic can be caused by sudden changes in lifestyle, such as feed, exercise and bedding. Horses, especially miniature horses, are very sensitive to change, and any sudden change can cause an upset stomach, but because horses are non-emetic, they cannot throw up. Horses with a heavy worm burden are more disposed to colic. It can also be caused by infections and blockages in the stomach or gut. For this reason, if the remedies explained here do not clear up colic, you should seek veterinary treatment. A vet may be able to treat the colic with a simple course of antibiotics, or your horse may need surgery. The sooner treatment is received, the more likely they will gain full recovery.

If you make sure you keep up to date with worming medications, your animal will be less likely to contract colic. Constant access to fresh, clean water will also reduce the risk of colic. If your horse is showing signs of mild colic, there are a few things you can do to relieve the discomfort. You should walk them for 10 minutes every half an hour and remove access to hay and feed, (not water) and make sure there is nothing your horse could hurt themselves on if they roll and let them have a lie down if they want – it is a fallacy that you should stop a horse with colic from lying down.

**Don't give your horse any medication without consulting your vet** as this can cover up symptoms, meaning you could think your horse has recovered. Keeping a logbook record of food and behaviour may make it easier to pinpoint the cause and start of the problem.

**Hyperlipidemia**

Hyperlipidemia is more common in overweight animals, but can occur in seemingly healthy animals. As miniature horses are more prone to over-eating than standard sized horses, they are more likely to suffer from hyperlipidemia.

Symptoms of hyperlipidemia include lethargy, weight loss and diarrhoea. It is very difficult to tell if your miniature horse has hyperlipidemia, for a number of reasons. One reason is that the symptoms are similar to those of other illnesses. Also, hyperlipidemia can be caused by other illnesses and be a secondary problem.

Hyperlipidemia is when excess fat is metabolized in response to reduced food intake. The lipids (fat) are released into the bloodstream. This then builds up in the liver cells and damages them. Treatment is putting the animal on a glucose drip and giving insulin. A vet would also need to find the underlying cause. As with many problems with the health of your miniature horse, keeping an accurate logbook record of food, water intake and behaviour may make it easier to pinpoint the cause and start of the problem.

**Fecalith impaction**

This is a progressive, non-responsive abdominal pain caused by a hard, impacted mass of faeces in the colon or intestine. If a horse is failing to defecate and is showing signs of abdominal pain, fecalith impaction should be considered as a possible cause.

If you suspect fecalith impaction, you must seek veterinary advice immediately, as surgical correction may be necessary, and the sooner any action is taken the more effective it will be and the better the outcome for your miniature horse. If you notice the signs early enough, an enema may be all it takes to remove the blockage, or it may be possible to remove the blockage without surgery. Whatever the case, any remedy should only be administered by your vet, or with their advice.

Miniature horses may be predisposed to fecalith impaction and as an owner you should be aware of this. Feed should be considered as a factor in any animal that has suffered fecalith impaction and their diet during recovery should be carefully controlled. Hay should contain less than 50% alfalfa as this is high in protein, wheat bran should be restricted and exercise should be encouraged. Horses disposed to fecalith impaction should be fed 2% -2.5% of their body weight in hay daily to clear their system out. Horses with dwarfism are at a higher risk of fecalith impaction.

**Narcolepsy**

Narcolepsy in horses is a very odd phenomenon whereby the horse will have episodes of uncontrollable loss of muscle tone (cataplexy) and sleep. It can occur at any time in a horse's life, from very young to mature adulthood. Horses with narcolepsy can sleep during grooming or even exercise. If your miniature hors isn't going to be ridden, which is usually the case, there is no problem with keeping a horse with narcolepsy.

The future for animals with this condition can vary greatly. Some horses with narcolepsy just grow out of it. Narcolepsy is very rare and there is no cure. This doesn't mean a horse with the condition can't live a happy and otherwise healthy life.

Miniature horses, along with thoroughbreds, are more likely to develop narcolepsy. There are some medical treatments for narcolepsy and if you're worried you should seek veterinary advice, although the medications currently available can be as damaging as they are useful, and as narcolepsy isn't life threatening, or even particularly distressing for a horse, there is very little point in treating them. However, discuss it with your vet.

Narcoleptic horses should not be ridden, especially by children. If your miniature horse has narcolepsy, they should be kept away from aggressive animals and sharp fence posts, other than that, there are no real safety concerns.

## Respiratory infections

Because of their high muscle content, large lungs, long windpipes, and large open nostrils horses are incredibly prone to a number of respiratory infections that can be quite distressing for both the horse and its owner. If your horse shows any signs of respiratory infection, seek veterinary advice.

## Strangles

Strangles is an incredibly infectious disease caused by bacteria called *Streptococcus equi*. The bacteria themselves are similar to the ones that cause strep throat in humans. *Streptococcus equi* get into the lymph nodes and can cause horrid pain. Spread by contact, direct horse to horse contact or indirect via bedding or human clothing, strangles causes depression, loss of appetite, and a high temperature. Sometimes the lymph nodes can get abscesses and ooze pus into the throat and mouth.

Treatment includes rest, intensive nursing and often antibiotics - though the use of antibiotics for strangles is controversial. If you suspect strangles, seek veterinary advice immediately. Animals with strangles need to be isolated as soon as you notice possible symptoms, as symptoms do not occur until 2-14 days, any other horses who have been in contact with them in the last 2 weeks should also be isolated and monitored. If you plan to show your horse or if your horse lives with animals that are shown or raced, you should have them vaccinated. To avoid the spread of strangles, animals known to be infected or to have been infected within the last 2 months should not be allowed into contact with uninfected animals and strict contamination procedures should be adhered to; bedding and food of infected/previously infected animals should not be shared, humans in contact with such animals should be aware of washing their hands and clothes between visits.

**Influenza**

Equine flu is very contagious and can affect any animal in the equine family – horse, donkey, even zebra. Because of this, containment and isolation is highly recommended. Horses with flu may have an elevated temperature, swollen glands, loss of appetite and depression, a dry cough that lasts a few weeks, stiff, painful joints and runny eyes. They may have some or all of these symptoms.

A horse suspected of having flu should be rested straight away. They should be kept out of the heat and the cold, so stabling them would be a good idea, as long as there is still access to fresh air. If there is not much air movement in the stables, they should be walked a couple of times a day, but not fast and not far, just enough to get fresh air into their lungs. They must be kept dry and warm, but not allowed to overheat. Try to avoid dust in their hay and feed. Once recovered, they should rest for about 3 weeks. If your horse races, though this is less likely for miniature horses, they need 2 months rest after having influenza in order for their respiratory tract to fully recover.

If you suspect influenza, seek veterinary advice and isolate any animals that may be infected as well as observing any that may have come into contact with infected animals.

## Arteritis

Equine viral arteritis, or EVA, is a highly contagious disease. EVA doesn't usually kill horses, but it can cause abortion in pregnant mares and death in young foals. It is spread in the same way as other respiratory infections and, as with the others, affected animals should be isolated and a vet should be called. There will often be no symptoms with EVA until the disease is at the acute stage.

Symptoms include fever, depression, dependent edema (liquid lumps and bumps under the skin where fluid builds up) localized or generalized hives or rash, runny eyes and nose. A pregnant mare with arteritis will often abort. When pregnant mares are exposed to the virus very close to term, they may not abort but give birth to an infected foal that will quickly develop pneumonia and die.

Horses that are not pregnant should be vaccinated against EVA. EVA can be treated with antibiotics and rest. Stallions who have been infected will often carry the disease and should only be bred to EVA positive mares or mares that are properly vaccinated (a horse is EVA positive if they have the antibodies for EVA).

## Herpesvirus

Equine Herpesvirus or Rhinopneumonitis can infect the throat, nose and lungs, causing loss of appetite, sluggishness and coughs and runny noses. It can also cause abortion in pregnant mares and neurological symptoms such as lack of coordination. This is an illness that usually affects younger horses and will often remain latent in the horse long after they have recovered until the virus reactivates when the animal is older.

There are no vaccines for the herpesvirus, so infected (or previously infected) horses should be monitored, as should any movement of infected (or previously infected) horses, and a good quarantine routine should be in place. If you feel there may be any risk at all of herpesvirus you should quarantine any animals involved or suspected to be involved and seek veterinary advice.

**Arthritis**

Arthritis is a painful, progressive and limiting illness that affects many of us. It can also affect horses. The symptoms are fairly obvious and are decreased range of movement and less willingness to move about as much.

There are treatments that can alleviate the pain, although there is not yet a cure. If your horse develops arthritis your vet will go through the various treatment options, and you should not consider arthritis the end of the animal's healthy life – they can still continue to have a good quality of life. The long-term prognosis for miniature horses is better than that of larger horses. Because there is less weight on the joints and less pressure on the feet, they tend to suffer less if they do contract arthritis. Also, as miniature horses are less likely to be riders or racers, the owners tend not to see it as the end of the horses usefulness.

**Septicaemia**

Septicaemia is a deadly bloodstream infection that can kill an animal very quickly. Septicemia is the presence of bacteria or bacterial toxins in the bloodstream, and can kill very quickly. As miniature horses are smaller, they will succumb to the infection even faster than larger horses. The higher risk of death makes this a very serious illness and you need to be constantly on the look out for septicaemia and seek veterinary advice as soon as you spot any signs, as early detection can literally be the difference between life and death. The younger the animal, the more danger it will be in, due to the weaker immune system. It is also far more likely in foals that have not had their colostrums.

There is no vaccination for this so you need to be very vigilant. It can often be treated with antibiotics, but not always, so prevention is the key. Any cuts, grazes or scrapes need to be treated with antiseptic cream and kept clean. This includes cuts in the mouth and splits in the hoof. Anywhere that any blood or flesh is in contact with the outside world needs to be kept clean. Unlike a lot of equine aliments, septicaemia isn't contagious by external contact.

## 2. How to tell if your miniature horse is under the weather

If your miniature horse becomes ill, spotting the signs as soon as possible and getting them to the vet could be the difference between life and death. Here are some signs to look out for:

**Weight loss**

If you notice any sudden, unexpected weight loss you should seek veterinary advice. This can be a symptom of all sorts of problems. As well as finding the underlying cause, the weight loss in itself can be incredibly damaging to the internal organs of the horse and can cause hyperlipidemia, where the body panics and releases stored fat into the blood. Even if you have put your miniature horse on a diet because they were overweight, sudden or dramatic weight loss may still be a cause for concern.

**Temperature change**

Any change in your horse's temperature can indicate a serious health problem, and you should seek veterinary advice immediately. The most serious health problems that a horse can develop have temperature change as a symptom. Any cooling can upset a horse in itself, and a raise in temperature can damage the organs.

**Suddenly becoming timid**

If your horse suddenly becomes timid, seek veterinary advice immediately. It could be that your horse is reacting to touch sensitivity by avoiding contact, or it could be a symptom of a neurological condition. Any change in behaviour should be monitored and if you are worried you should always call your vet.

## 3. Grooming and health

A good grooming regime can do wonders for keeping your horse healthy. Brushing and checking your miniature horse regularly will quickly acquaint you with their body. Knowing the normal muscle tone, temperature and general condition of your horse will make it easy to pick up on any potential problems as soon as symptoms arise. As with all health issues, early detection and diagnosis makes treatment much simpler and recovery quicker and more likely.

## Hoofs

The hooves should be kept trimmed and clean. Lots of people do this themselves, though you should have some training (formal or informal) before attempting this. Another popular option is a farrier. Farriers are very knowledgeable about the foot health of horses and a good farrier will pick up on any problems as soon as they are developing, reducing the illness itself as well as the treatment requirements and the distress for both horse and owner. If there is any discomfort in walking, this is usually caused by something wrong with the hoof. Ask a farrier or seek veterinary advice as soon as possible, as any problems with the hoof can leave a horse lame and in excruciating pain.

## Teeth

A horse's teeth need to be checked regularly. Because horses' teeth continue to grow, they can grow into the sides of the mouth and cause discomfort that can stop the horse from eating properly. The teeth can also rot in the head, causing discomfort and pain. If there is any discomfort or pain in the mouth for any reason, a horse can stop eating. This can lead to dramatic weight loss, hyperlipidemia and muscle wastage. It has been known for horses to starve to death because of a bad tooth. If the horse seems to have something wrong with its teeth, seek veterinary advice.

**Fur and skin**

A horse's fur and skin should be kept clean and refreshed by regular grooming. This can also help you to keep an eye on any changes in condition that may occur and will improve the animal's general heath and wellbeing. The fur and skin should be in good, regular condition, with no flaking, bald patches, external parasites or lesions. If you notice any of these signs and are not sure of their cause or correct treatment, seek veterinary advice.

## 4. When to take your miniature horse to the vet

A lot of little niggles and things that might worry your miniature horse will need treating, but not always by a vet. Most scrapes and scratches and a little cold should be treated immediately to avoid infections, but you can usually do this yourself. There are times, however, when veterinary intervention is absolutely vital. There are also times when it's hard to say- they might not *need* to see the vet but it's always better safe than sorry.

A good rule of thumb is, when in doubt, seek veterinary advice. Even if you've been told by friends or neighbours, or even books, that you don't need to see a vet, if you are still unsure, phone them. They may reassure you over the phone that it's fine, or they may come out and save the horse's life.

**Becoming unresponsive**

If for any reason your miniature horse becomes unresponsive, you must seek veterinary advice as soon as possible. Not responding to noise can suggest ear infections, deafness or head trauma. Ignoring the sight and movement of those around it can suggest any number of illnesses, including infections, problems with eyesight and physical distress.

**Thirst or hunger**

Excessive thirst or hunger can be a sign of all sorts of horrid things, such as poisoning, diabetes and infections. Don't panic immediately though. The first thing that you need to check is whether or not your miniature horse has had access to enough clean water. If not, that could explain why they are so thirsty. If they have not had access to water for some time you may still want to consult your vet, as dehydration can make animals very poorly. But if there was sufficient water and they drank it all, and continued to be thirsty, this could mean your animal is unwell. Seek veterinary advice.

**Poison**

Horses cannot vomit – they are completely non-emetic. If your horse has ingested something you know or even suspect to be poisonous, or even if you only think they may have, you must seek veterinary advice immediately. Horses cannot get rid of anything in their stomachs because they are non-emetic. Sometimes the body may try to expel poisons through diarrhoea, though this can also be dangerous in itself. It can't be stressed enough how helpless horses, of all sizes, are against poisons.

**Seizure**

If your miniature horse has any sort of seizure, no matter how small, go to the vet. A seizure can look like a small, sudden collapse that seems quickly recovered from or it can be a collapse followed by a worrying time of incapacity and possibly shaking. It can also be very subtle, with all of the muscles tensing up and the horse becoming rigid. Most animals suffering from a seizure will evacuate their bowels. If you suspect a seizure, seek veterinary advice.

**Strange movement**

If your miniature horse begins to move strangely and you can't see a reason, i.e. they don't like their new bridle or they're not used to walking with a head collar, seek veterinary advice. Strange movements can be an indication of neurological problems, or it could be an early indication of narcolepsy. Strange movements can also be associated with physical discomfort. A horse with arthritis, colic or any bone or muscle damage will need treating immediately. It could also just be a hoof that needs cleaning better.

**Fur loss**

Fur loss is often indicative of a lice infestation or poor health and condition. If you are confident that your miniature horse does not have any external parasites, you should seek veterinary advice for both treatment of the fur loss and the underlying cause.

**Lumps and bumps**

If you feel an abnormal lump, it isn't necessarily cancer, but you need to seek immediate veterinary help, as even a benign fat lump can make your miniature horse uncomfortable or ill. Other lumps may be fluid trapped underneath the skin; this is called dependent edema and could be a sign of arteritis, a very serious illness. Any bruises should be looked at and the cause of any bruising should be investigated and, where possible, removed.

## Bleeding

Any profuse bleeding, obviously, needs to be seen by the vet. A little scratch will usually be ok, but even a small cut can become infected and an infection needs to be treated by the vet before septicaemia sets in. You should have an antiseptic rub in your emergency kit. If a small cut takes a long time to heel, you can treat it with styptic. You should also have styptic in your emergency kit.

## Laminitis

Acute laminitis is a medical emergency. Go to the vet. Recovery is quicker, cheaper and lasts longer the sooner treatment is received. You will often find that a good farrier will have advice for interim treatment until a vet can be contacted. Any laminitis needs to be treated urgently, as it is horrifically painful, and failure to treat this condition can lead to permanent damage to the feet, legs and even hip/shoulder joints.

## Broken bones

This is very obvious but any serious injury or wound of any kind needs veterinary help. If you even suspect any broken bones, your miniature horse needs urgent veterinary attention.

**Discharge from the eyes or nose**

This could be a symptom of a serious respiratory illness, or just a little sniffle. It's always better safe than sorry and if your miniature horse does have a respiratory infection, the sooner it is treated the better. If any discharge continues for more than a couple of days, is excessive, contains any blood or is coupled with any other symptoms you should seek veterinary advice.

## 5. Diets and vaccinations to keep your miniature horse healthy

Going on and on about keeping a logbook may be annoying, but it saves so much time and worry. If you keep- in your logbook- a record of the vaccination schedule, any treatments or illnesses and the animals diet, behaviour and any treats given, it can be a lot easier to pinpoint any dietary causes of problems or illnesses. Some horses are sensitive to certain types of grass or grain so a record of food and mood can show up any correlations and the problem might be very easily fixed.

## 6. Finding a vet

One of the most important things to do before anything goes wrong is to find a vet. The best way to find yourself a vet is to ask people who already own miniature horses, if you are buying your mini locally, then your breeder should be able to recommend a good vet, if they can't you may want to reconsider where you get him/her from.

Ask at local pony clubs, or on online forums. Phone around local veterinary surgeries, you may find a small animal vet actually specialised in horses. If you already have a horse, ask your current equine vet, as they will often look after minis as well.

# 7. *Emergency kit*

There are a few things you should have on hand with any pet. With most pets you can get the things you'll need in an emergency quite readily at a local store or supermarket. Miniature horses, however, are not very common pets, and should the occasion arise, there are a few things you should have in case of an emergency. An animal first aid kit is an old idea, but a good one.

### Styptic

Styptic is a clotting agent used by used all sorts of people for all sorts of reasons. Men use it when they cut themselves shaving; rabbit owners use it when they cut the claws too short. When sprinkled on small cuts that bleed for too long, styptic is a fantastic clotting aid and can help a wound heel quickly, avoiding infection. It comes in stick form for human use, but is also available as a powder, such as Kwik-Stop Styptic Powder and works out at about $10 or £7 an ounce. Most horse owners won't use anywhere near that in an animals lifetime.

### Animalintex Poultice

Any sort of medicated hoof poultice can be very useful for hoof abscesses. As soon as you notice something wrong with your horse's hoof, you can clean the dirt out and apply the poultice to protect and seal the hoof until you can get a vet in to look at it. If the vet could be a few days, you should change the dressing daily. This will draw out the infection. You can find detailed instructions for this on youtube, on forums or on the packaging.

**Antiseptic**

An antiseptic gel like Radiol B-R antibacterial Jelly or a spray like Purple Spray can help avoid all sorts of problems. Applied directly and immediately to any minor cuts, scrapes and grazes, an anti-bacterial agent can stop infections occurring, potentially saving hundreds, if not thousands in veterinary bills, as well as a lot of pain and distress for your miniature horse. Any infections should be treated immediately by the vet to avoid septicaemia, and any real wounds need to be looked at by a vet anyway.

**Electrolyte compound**

Keeping a compound of electrolytes handy could well save your horse's life if they ever develop any diarrhoea or dehydration. When your horse is ill, they could easily become dehydrated and die of dehydration rather than the initial illness.

**Probiotics**

Because of the complex nature of horse digestion, it is important that their gut flora is kept healthy. If there has been any problem with digestion, whether it be sudden weight loss or just a small bout of diarrhoea, replacing the 'good' bacteria and promoting its health in the animal's gut is vitally important.

# Chapter 8) Play and enrichment

## *1. Games*

There are so many lovely games to play with your miniature horse.

**Hide and seek**

Miniature horses love to play hide and seek. If there are trees in their paddock they will hide behind them, or you can hide behind the trees, peeking out until they come to investigate you. Then dip further round the tree, letting them see you and find you sometimes to keep their interest. They really like this cheeky little game.

**Football (soccer)**

Miniature horses won't play football in the same way larger horses will, as they tend not to have a rider to encourage them to go for the ball. But if you have a few miniature horses in a field together and they are all interested in the ball, they will chase the ball, kicking it away from each other and tackling each other.

**Fetch**

Balls with handles on are so much fun as they can be kicked about or picked up and carried. If you throw or kick the ball away, once your miniature horse is interested in the ball, they will rush after it, frolicking about.

## 2. Toys

Horses are intelligent animals and are easily bored. A bored animal is an unhappy animal, and as an owner it is your responsibility to keep your miniature horse happy. You can't be with them all of the time, but you can and should provide entertainment.

There is a wide range of toys available to keep miniature horses occupied. A lot of these toys will involve a food treat. You can use this as an opportunity to give your horse some much needed dietary supplements. You can get toy compatible treats that contain all sorts of things, from salt licks to cod-liver oil. Many owners also use these treat toys to administer wormer and other medications.

### a) Bought toys

There are lots of websites that sell boredom busters for horses. These clever companies make all sorts of food-based enrichment toys that can keep your horse entertained when you're not around.

### Hanging likit holder

There are all sorts of hanging holders for salt licks and treats out there. They are a fantastic way to keep your miniature horse entertained and healthy, as you can use them to introduce electrolytes, vitamins and other dietary supplements. These devices hang from the ceiling and contain delicious things that are good for your horse and that they want to lick. Because it is hanging, it moves around and the horse will have to move their head and neck about to taste and bite their treat. This provides a nice bit of mental exercise.

**Tongue twister**

The tongue twister is a similar thing to the hanging holder, but it can be attached to the stable wall or to fence posts and trees. It holds the treat and the horse has to twist their tongue around to get at it. The device doesn't move about but its components do, moving and getting in the way of the enquiring tongue and making the horse think and move about.

**Boredom Breaker**

This is a clever hanging toy with a hanging lickit holder and a ball suspended from the bottom of the string. The ball has a compartment for more treats and because the ball turns around, the treats aren't always at the front for the horse to access, so the horse has to use their mind a bit to get at their treat.

**Boredom buster**

This is very similar to the boredom breaker, except that the ball not only rotates horizontally, but also vertically. Most of these toys can be hung off of each other and made into even more interesting, complicated devices.

**Treat balls**

The Snak-a-ball (http://www.likit.co.uk/) or Pasture Pal (http://www.equi-spirit-toys.com) or Nose-It (http://www.nose-it.com) are very similar to treat balls for smaller animals and can be filled with whatever feed you use for your miniature horse. It roles around on the ground and the horse nudges it to move it about. The food falls out of the hole in small amounts for the horse to eat. This is excellent because not only does it keep your miniature horse occupied, it also keeps the food relatively clean while encouraging natural grazing behaviours, which have a beneficial effect on the mental wellbeing of animals in captivity.

**Balls**

There is a whole range of balls for horses to play with, from traditional footballs (soccer balls) to balls with handles that they can carry about with them. The amazing thing is that horses will play with these with very little encouragement, and if left alone with them, will play with them whenever they want.

**b) Home made toys and how to make them**

Things with the word "horse" in front of them will often come with a high price tag, but that doesn't mean you can't keep your horse entertained without breaking the bank, as there are all sorts of toys you can make yourself.

**Ice-lolly**

On very hot days, your horse needs to keep cool. A good way to help them do this is to chop up some of their favourite fruits and veggies and freeze them in a block of water. Old ice cream or margarine tubs make good ice trays and make ice-lollies of about the right size. Ice should only be given on very hot days and only in small amounts. It should also be supervised, I'm not saying stand there and watch until it's all eaten up, but someone should be around if your miniature horse is being given a frozen treat to cool down.

## Rattle

Horses like to be able to control their environment as much as possible. They also love making noise. A plastic bottle with a handle, like the ones you get milk in, with nuts or pebbles can make a really good rattle. Suspended from the rafters, it will be a great thing for your horse to head butt around, or throw it on the floor to be kicked about and stomped on.

## Hanging bottle treat

Or if you choose you can make a treat bottle in the same way, with holes on the bottom or the lid left off and hung up. The horse will have to really work at it to make the treats come out.

## Hay hanger

If you hang your hay in hay nets, try suspending them from the rafters so that the horse has to work at getting the hay out as the bundle moves and sways.

## Grazing roller

Or you can tie hay around a drainpipe with strong jute or hemp string. Wrap a lot round and tie great big handfuls of it on. Then you can leave it with your horse to graze from. This way, it will roll out of reach, making your miniature horse work a little harder for their dinner.

## Carrot ball

Take a net with a smaller hole size, then tie it around an old ball, a soccer ball or a basket ball with some of the air out of it. Leave some room in the net. Then you can stuff carrots into the gaps until they cover the ball. Then, hang the carrot ball in the stalls, not too close to the walls, for your horse to help themselves to.

**Dinner hanger**

Hanging their food is a great way to keep your horse entertained while they are indoors overnight. There are lots of ways to do this, but wrapping the regular feed up with a few treats and binding it in hay is a great way to do it. If you bind the hay tight with jute or hemp, the food will be bound up and difficult to get at, providing a little extra challenge with dinner.

**Bobbing for apples**

All you need is a large water container barrel and some apples. This is a really fun game for your horse and they can be left to play with this on their own.

**Home made feed-ball**

Horses love to kick things about and you can use any large container, such as a 2-litre drinks bottle or a gallon milk bottle, to make your own feed-ball. If you drill a few holes in the side and leave the lid off you can fill the container with treats and leave the lid off to avoid choking. Your miniature horse will love kicking this about and foraging for the tasty things that escape.

**Play rope**

The rope or string stays put and every day or every other day you change what you hang from the rope. It could be as easy and simple as a plastic milk jug, you can find some nice hard rubber dog toys, and even plastic bowls of different shapes or colours. The ideal height depends on the horse's height. You would want to hang it so that the hanging item can just touch his back. My guys love to walk under some of the toys to try and scratch their backs & others like to pull on it. Some days you don't want to hang anything. The idea is to keep it interesting and see what you can come up with that is relatively safe.

**Basketball bag**

A hanging basketball will provide a good head-butting toy. They'll batter it about if you hang it at head height. This is a really great game for them to get out any pent up aggression. They might rear up to kick at it though, so you shouldn't hang it anywhere low down.

**Kick bottle**

Bottles filled with treats make great kick toys. Just leave the lid off to avoid any risk of chocking on it and to let some of the treats come out. This should release the food only after some effort and scatter it randomly, encouraging natural foraging and grazing behaviour.

**Paper bags/cardboard boxes**

This isn't technically a made toy, but horses of all sizes love paper bags and scrunched up newspaper to make a game. They toss them in the air and chase them and tear at them and have such fun! Boxes with any staples and tape removed are used in the same way, but will last a little longer before they have been torn up completely.

## Rummage box

A rummage box is a spectacular idea for a horse toy. Take an old draw or something similar and fill it with largish, smooth pebbles so no noses or tongues get grazed. Then just pop in pieces of apple/treats in amongst the pebbles and the horse spends quite a while working his mouth around the pebbles to find the treats.

## An old tire.

Tires are fun and durable and make great toys. Given a tire, a horse will toss it around for hours, and this is especially exciting if there is another horse interested in playing as well, as they can chase each other about. You can wedge food into the rims of tires and let the horse drag it about the paddock and spread their dinner out.

## Willow branches

Willow branches make great chews for miniature horses. They absolutely love willow. Horses know what's good for them and willow kills worms and thins the blood, which stops it building up in the hooves. Thinner blood doesn't clog in the tiny capillaries in the hooves, reducing the likelihood of laminitis. Not only is willow good for your horse, but they love it too. Many riders include a willow stop on their rout.

You can buy most of these things on eBay, but you can also pick these things up at supermarkets, second hand shops and scrap yards.

# Chapter 9) Training your miniature horse

Why train your horse?

If you train your horse with a few basic ideas your life will be a lot easier. It will make them easier to handle and easier to deal with in general. Training your horse will also be an enjoyable way to spend time with them.

**The basics**

**Coming When Called**

Give your miniature horse its favourite treat while saying its name over and over again. Do this daily and hopefully your miniature horse will come to you for a treat! Make sure that when the horse comes to you, you do reward it each and every time!

**Biting**

If your miniature horse gets into a habit of getting what they want by biting you, then they will continue to do so. If you pull away when your horse bites, then they will think they are in charge. They need to know that no one is in charge, but that no one is submissive.

The main thing to do if your horse bites is to understand *why* they have bitten. Could it be that they were just showing affection? In the wild, horses nibble at the top of each other's mane. Is it because they have been spooked by something and they are trying to get your attention or comfort? Or are they genuinely being aggressive?

If they are trying to show affection, you need to show them a more appropriate way. Teach them to show affection by nuzzling instead.

If they are spooked, put a firm hand on their neck and show them that they are safe.

If they are being aggressive, you need to be firm. Put your hand on their nose and push their face down –not so hard or firm as to hurt them, just enough to let them know that you won't stand for that sort of behaviour. Stand up straight and show them that you are bigger. It is important that you do not loose your temper at any point. If you loose your temper and make your animal afraid of you, it can take a very long time to regain their trust once you have broken it.

**Showing hooves**

Teaching your horse to be calm and stand still while you inspect each hoof will save time and reduce stress when it comes to checking and trimming hooves.

First, calm your horse, and stand next to him/her, still and firm. If there is anyone with you, ask him or her to calm your horse at their face, feeding them treats. If there is no one with you, stand your horse by their food trough, so that they are distracted and calm. The main event shouldn't be their feet being lifted and checked. If the most important thing that is happening is the food, that is what they will care about. Hold the foot for a very short time at first, increasing the time as you go on. If you normalize the foot inspection by repeating this action as often as possible, then when the time comes to have the hooves rasped or trimmed there will be no fear involved.

## Spooking

If your horse spooks easily, you need to work out what, specifically, is frightening them. Animals, especially prey animals, are very aware of their surroundings, and things that they don't know or understand could easily be trying to eat them. If they are frightened of tarps or bags on posts, you need to introduce them to these things in a safe, controlled environment.

One owner found that her horses loved playing bobbing for apples. So one night she put the bobbing for apples barrel in their paddock, as usual, but this time it was on top of a tarp that they had been frightened of. It was laid flat on the floor, with the barrel on top of it. In the morning, the apples had been eaten and the tarp wasn't so frightening anymore. Then, when they rode past tarpaulins in the future, the animals weren't afraid of them any more.

One owner had horses that were frightened of people riding bikes. So he left an old bike in the stables, out of reach the first few nights, then where they could get at it. They could investigate the bike in a safe, controlled environment. They found that it wasn't anything to be worried about. Then he rode past the field on a bike, slowly and unthreatening. Soon the horses were used to bikes and wouldn't spook around them anymore.

Find out what spooks your horse and normalise it, allowing them to understand that whatever it is that upsets them is not a real threat to their safety. Once a horse understands this, they will be much calmer in general.

## Head-shy

If your horse is head-shy, it could become dangerous. Not out of malice, but out of fear. They are frightened that something is going to hurt their face.

There are a number of ways to treat head-shy horses, but the best ways do not use pain or force, as this will only reinforce their fear.

Many recommend letting the horse get used to having things touch their heads on their own terms. A good way to do this is letting the horse play games with hanging toys. Having hanging ball toys for them to move about with their head in their own time will teach them that they are stronger than they thought, and that their faces aren't as sensitive as they thought.

There are lots of stories about head-shy horses being stalled with a hanging basketball and battering it about all night with their head. Head-shy horses need time, patience and understanding.

## Guide horses for the blind

Guide horses for the blind are fantastically well trained and the people who train them are very specialized. They are trained to assist in the same way that guide dogs are. They live long and are strong and have good stamina.

**Show jumping**

Training your horse to show jump is a long but rewarding process. It is important that you be realistic about your ambitions and capabilities as well as the ability of your horse so as not to put undue stress or pressure on either of you.

Once your horse walks comfortably with a halter, you should teach them to trot alongside you as you run with it. At this point you should set out a small course of small jumps. Approach them at a decent pace, encouraging them to jump over each one as it comes.

Increase the size of the jumps slowly over time, being aware of the comfort zone of your horse. As your horse is comfortable with the current height of jump, you can progress onto the next. Not before though. Don't push for too much improvement too fast, as your horse will know what you want from them and will not want to disappoint you.

**Pony and trap**

Introduce your horse to the trap slowly. You should do this one component at a time and only to the point where your horse is comfortable, then remove the components. The first few times your miniature horse pulls anything, you should be right there next to their head, keeping them calm and reassuring them.

**Dog tricks**

It may seem odd, but you can teach your miniature horse to do 'dog' tricks.

It is important to use distinct sounds and that they are recognizable in your voice, and commands should be short words with easily identifiable sounds so that your horse can understand what is expected of it.

When teaching a new horse to sit, people tend to use "sit" where the main sound is the 'it' at the end, concentrating on the hard 't'. Like with dogs, it is easier if you use the hand signal of an upward facing flat palm and bring your hand up towards your face, or moving the hand over the head and back. There is a fascination with the treat on top of your hand. Your horse will watch to see where the goodies are.

For teaching the horse to wait, whether before it eats its food, at roads or when it hass wandered off too far on a walk, I use "stop" where the main sound is the 'op' at the end of the word. The hand signal I use for this is a hand facing outwards like a traffic warden. This is a piece of training that should be taught on a long tether at first, with the command being given if the horse stops of their own accord, or before stopping the slack on the tether.

Stay is a different command, as I will be walking away from the horse and not towards it; here I use "stay" where the main sound is 'ay'. I use the same hand signal for this as I use for stop.

To call the horse I will say "come" in a higher pitched, clipped voice, so that is it one quick sound. Hand signals aren't very useful here.

Laying down is not a necessary skill for a horse, but can be useful. I say "lie", as it is a quite short sound. The usual hand signal for this is a flat palm facing down, moving towards the ground in a smooth motion. Your horse may well be disinclined to lie down. If they don't want to lie down, don't make them.

To get the horse to let go of something or put it down I say "drop" where the main sound is the 'ro' in the middle of the word. I point at the horse.

# Chapter 10) Assistance animals and famous minis

Miniature horses have hit the headlines all over the world lately for a variety of reasons. There have been a number of tiny horses in the news, mostly for their size, with specific littlies such as Einstein, Beau and Vita being in the papers and all over YouTube for their smallness alone. Others, like Rosie, Henry and Larry have been noticed for their skills and if you type miniature horse tricks into YouTube you will find a wide variety of very cute videos and images of miniature horses showing off. Another famous mini is Mr P the therapy horse. One of the most impressive reasons that miniature horses have been in the news, though, is that they are now being used as assistance animals – guide horses for the blind!

Einstein was born in 2010 and was the smallest foal ever to survive. At 6lbs, he was comparable in size to a human baby and in order to keep him warm he had to have a Jack Rustle dog coat, as there were no horse blankets for sale small enough for him. Despite his small size, there is no evidence that Einstein has dwarfism. He lives with some female goats, which he can often be seen herding about with, keeping them safe from other boys!

Beau has also become an internet sensation, with almost a million views of his video, "Adorable Beau", where he is seen strutting his stuff, playing with soft toys, a cat and various balls.

Vita is the smallest miniature horse in Scotland and is not only small, but very sweet natured. She stands at 25 inches and is a European miniature horse. She has lived in a custom-built stable and is a real hit with visitors to her owner's coffee shop. She also goes to a lot of charity fundraising events with her little friend Merlin (also a European miniature) where they both get a lot of fuss. The gentle, calm nature of miniature horses makes them perfect for this sort of high crowd situation.

Rosie the miniature horse is a wonderful example of a well-trained horse enjoying her tricks. She can open Velcro, play the triangle and the xylophone, stack dishes, place hoops over a stick (very useful, eh?) and do all manner of funny walks. She will also sit, lie down and roll on command. She is very good at ball games and tidying up. Her video is "miniature horse does dog tricks" and it is a very good example of how horses can be trained using nothing but positive reinforcement.

Henry has grown up into a therapy animal with the Riley's Place program, but in his younger days he was quite the footballer, running around after a ball bigger than him in a very funny video.

**Larry**

The British horse Mr P is a fantastic example of how animals can provide comfort and therapy to people. Mr P, who is only 29 inches tall, has been nominated for a care award for his work with older people in Durham. The calm nature and sweet stature of these horses means that they are ideally suited to providing a stable form of calm and relaxation.

Because of their small stature, gentle and calm nature and ease of care, miniature horses are being promoted as guide animals for the blind. They are also more suitable for those with a fear of dogs or dog hair allergies. According to The Guide Horse Foundation, horses are "natural guide animals" with "natural guide instincts".

This idea that they are naturally adapted to guiding the blind comes from wild horses. In wild or feral populations, if a horse goes blind, another horse will become its guide, keeping it safe within the herd, guiding it to food and water and away from danger. The sighted horse will become completely responsible for the welfare of the blind horse.

As prey animals, horses are much more danger aware than dogs, and are constantly on the look out for potential hazards and are very good at avoiding obstacles, not only for themselves, but for their blind person or 'herd'.

Because of their much longer life expectancy, 30-40 years, guide horses would make more sense as a life-long assistant than the relatively short lived dog.

Due to the shape of a horse's head, they can see at both sides and because of their amazing ability to move their eyes independently of each other, they can track a number of danger sources at the same time.

They are less likely to become distracted by food or crowds, as, unlike dogs, they are not very interested in either, as long as they are kept well fed. They do not crave human attention in the same way that dogs do, so are less likely to be distracted by a child petting them.

Like dogs, horses can be house trained. Unlike dogs, they do not get fleas and only shed a couple of times a year, meaning they don't make a mess.

Because horses are very trainable and can cope with more than 20 voice commands, they make excellent guide animals.

# Chapter 11) Breeding

If you own a male miniature horse that is strong and healthy and are interested in hiring him out to stud, there is little stopping you. You need to talk to an experienced breeder for advice about this and you could possibly get help from a local stud farm.

If you own a female miniature horse that is strong and healthy and are interested in breeding, however, there is a lot more to take into consideration. There are a lot of things to worry about and a bad pregnancy or birth could kill your horse.

Seek and accept advice from current horse breeders who have an excellent reputation with other horse breeders; check with your local horse association for more information. Most breeders will be happy to share information, as they're as keen as you to maintain high quality standards and to see more healthy horses.

# 1. Are you prepared for breeding your miniature horses?

Rearing a foal means extra work, and demands special facilities, including separate accommodation for the foal when it is weaned.

Once you have decided to breed and have quality horses to breed you need to do your research on the breeding process and risks associated with breeding so you are ready for anything. There are a number of things that can go wrong during breeding and it is better to be prepared than have the worst happen and no way to cope.

**Costs**

You need to pay for all sorts of things when you're planning on breeding your horse. There will be a need for high quality food. Regular vet visits are a must. The amount of time and effort invested in observing your mare has to be a consideration before you decide to breed.

**Insurance**

One thing you need to take into account is that your insurance may be invalidated by a pregnancy. You'd need to contact your insurer to find out where you stand. They might have a special pregnancy cover, but they might not. Just not telling the insurance company isn't really an option as someone would notice. Your insurance may be affected for some time after the birth as well.

**Dangers**

There are all sorts of infections that can kill the foetus before it is even born. A pregnant mare can become erratic and her behaviour may change permanently.

Pregnancy of young mares can hinder their growth, so you need to make sure your miniature horse is old enough. Coming into heat isn't necessarily a sign that she is physically prepared to have a baby.

Multiple foals- twins – can weaken the mare a lot and often only one, if any, will survive.

A prolapsed uterus can kill a horse very easily, and you should have a vet look at your mare to check her over, as it could take up to 3 weeks of care to nurse her back to health, and without this she could die.

If your miniature horse mum is eating and behaving normally then everything is probably fine, although, as they are essentially prey animals, they tend not to advertise any potential problems.

Any number of complications in pregnancy or birth could do some real damage, or even kill both mother and foal.

**Legal ramifications**

You are legally responsible for the foal even before they are born, and you are legally required to provide adequate care for them. Before you can sell your foal you will need to get them a passport.

## How to (getting pregnant)

A good way of telling if a mare is in heat is to put her in a padded stall with a 'teaser' stallion in the padded stall next to her. If the mare moves her tail to one side and sidles her rump towards the stallion, that means she's probably in heat. However, if she starts lashing out at the stallion, that means she probably is *not* in heat.

A typical heat cycle will be between 5 and 7 days once every 21 days and a mare will begin to cycle about a week after foaling. The most unique aspect of the mare's heat cycle is that she only ovulates about 24 to 48 hours before the end of the cycle.

## Pregnancy

The typical gestation period of a miniature mare is the same as for a standard sized horse - about 330 days, give or take 2 weeks. Some mares will foal at ten months whereas others will carry their baby for a full twelve months.

Once the mare is bred it is crucial to have a health maintenance program. The mare should be wormed regularly and it is very important to have a reliable vet that can give you advice when needed or is available if something goes wrong. If you are taking a mare to a different stallion to be bred, the stallion's owner will let you know what vaccinations are necessary and what preliminary measures you will have to take before the breeding. If you wish, you can have the mare pregnancy tested 14 days after breeding but a positive pregnancy test does not insure a live foal. Many things can happen over the course of the pregnancy.

## Foaling

Giving birth is dangerous for any animal, and your mare should be observed during this time. She will want to be alone, however, and won't want to have any human contact so you should quietly watch from a distance and wait.

It is best not to disturb the mare until she is finished foaling. The foaling process will take from 5 to 20 minutes. A balloon like sack will appear first and break, letting the fluids out. If the mare is having difficulties or a back leg is coming first you should seek veterinary help immediately. Most mares will handle it well and nature takes over and they know exactly what to do. However, some mares will not get the sack off the foal and you will need to assist in tearing the sack so the foal can breathe properly. If the sack has torn and the foal is breathing, leave the mare and foal alone to bond. The foal should start to stand in about 15 minutes, sometimes before the mare, and the umbilical cord and sack should break once the foal starts moving about. If it does not, simply tie it off with string about one and a half inches bellow the belly and cut it with scissors and disinfect the umbilical cord.

## Early baby care

Some of these foals may need special care. A premature foal will be smaller and need special attention but the overdue foal may have joint problems and need assistance to walk properly.

Foals need their mothers and should not be interfered with wherever possible. Observe them, yes, by all means keep a very close eye on your new baby.

You should make sure your mare is well fed and kept safe, warm and dry. This should be enough to keep your foal healthy and happy.

## 2. *Special dietary requirements*

Pregnant mares need high quality nutrition. Usually, for the first eight months of pregnancy, most mares can maintain themselves on good pasture, with lots of good quality hay and with minimal supplementary feed.

If your mare is overweight, she shouldn't be bread until she's lost some weight, but if she does fall pregnant while she's fat, you shouldn't try to make them loose weight. Putting them on a diet during pregnancy can radically increase the risk of abortion.

Because your foetus will double in size during the last 90 days of pregnancy, increased levels of energy, protein, minerals and vitamins are essential to support the growth of the foal, to maintain the condition of the mare and to prepare for lactation.

You should up the intake of protein, fibre, vitamins and minerals. Many feed sellers will sell special feed for pregnant mares.

## 3. *Specific housing*

While your mare can live in the same stable while pregnant and with her foal, you will need to keep the area free of any potential hazards, including other horses. An inquisitive other horse could damage the foal or spook the mother, causing *her* to damage the foal.

## 4. Looking after mum and baby

Keeping nutrition high and the wind out is the main thing you can do to keep mum and baby safe and healthy. You should watch the baby. They should be on their feet and feeding within 2-3 hours. The mother will be very attached to them very quickly and should provide any care they need.

If the foal is early, struggles to breath, took more than 40 minutes to birth, if the mare won't allow the baby to nurse or they take longer than 3 hours to be born they may well be in trouble. At this point you need to call your vet for help.

## 5. Embryo transfer

Embryo transfer is a relatively new technique that is similar to surrogacy in humans. The dam will become pregnant in the usual way and the embryo is implanted in a surrogate.

This is quite a risky procedure for the embryo. It is far safer for the biological mother, however, and is often the preferred method for prized horses and very important mares, whose owners do not want to risk their horse but do want to breed from them.

## 6. What to do if the mother rejects the babies

If your horse rejects her baby you need to act fast. Without the protection of their mother the foal could die very quickly. Try to reintroduce the foal.

If this fails, or if your mare dies in labour, contact all of the horse breeders you can. Try to find a lactating mare to foster the baby. They will often take another mare's foal if the foal is abandoned.

If you cannot find another mare to feed your foal, you need to keep them as warm as possible. They can drink goat's milk and you can even get hold of goat's colostrums and should have this at hand before your foal is born.

The milk should be warmed but not burnt and cows milk is not appropriate, even, as some claim, so called 'scolded' cows milk. This will make little foal tummies very upset. So you have your warm goat's milk, in the bottle. Always feed your horse standing up, if they are lying down they may drown.

NEVER feed a baby foal if it is cold. This can kill the foal, putting all your hard work and heartache to waste.

# Chapter 12) Miniature horses, the law and insurance

Before you get your miniature horse, you need to know where you stand with the law and licensing.

## 1. What licences do you need in your country?

**UK**

You currently do not need a licence to own or breed miniature horses in the UK.

If you are keeping horses on your own land, it needs to be registered. You need a County Parish Holding number (CPH) to keep agricultural animals, and even if they are miniature, horses are still counted as agricultural animals.

In the UK a horse needs a passport in order to allow them to be transported. It also allows a horse to be medicated and keeps the horse out of the food chain.

You need a Certificate of Competence if you are being paid to move horses or if you are moving horses to sell.

**USA**

In the USA it varies from state to state as to whether or not you need a licence to keep or move your horses.

In the USA a passport will be needed for competition. These competition passports must be renewed every 4 years.

## 2. *What are your legal responsibilities?*

**UK**

Under UK law you are responsible for the health and well being of your animal. You are responsible for the nutritional needs of your animal.

It is an offence not to provide adequate food and water.

It is an offence not to provide access to shelter.

It is an offence to allow your animal to live in unclean conditions.

It is an offence to go away without making provisions for the care of an animal.

It is an offence to intentionally harm an animal or to knowingly allow an animal to come to harm.

It is an offence not to provide adequate veterinary care.

If you are having financial difficulties, this is no excuse, but the RSPCA and PDSA may be able to help out.

**USA**

According to the animal welfare act of 1996, owners have legal responsibilities to their animals.

It is an offence to allow an animal to remain in pain.

It is an offence to deny, purposefully or by omition, access to adequate food and water.

It is an offence to cause pain or distress or allow pain or distress to be caused.

You must comply with humane end points. (Humane end points are chosen to minimize or terminate the pain or distress of the experimental animals via euthanasia rather than waiting for their deaths as the end point.)

## 3. Should you insure your pets?

The simple answer here is yes. You definitely should have your pet insured unless you have instant access to a few grand that you could spare on medical bills, should your miniature horse become ill or have an accident.

# Chapter 13) Buying your miniature horse

## *1. Where to get miniature horses*

Choosing where to get your miniature horse can be as important as choosing the horse itself. The main thing to consider is what you want from your animal. The information in this part of the book is fairly general, and you'll be able to find more specific information on where to get your miniature horse locally to you from local miniature horse owners. I strongly recommend joining forums and other online communities to get advice and support on specific things local to you.

### a) Auctions

Horse auctions are not for the faint hearted. If you choose to go down this route with your first miniature horse, it is a good idea to have someone with you who knows about horses. If you're friendly with an equine vet, that would be ideal, but if not, try to make friends with a horse owner local to you, or from one of the forums. Buying a miniature horse at auction has a lot of risks associated with it, but can also be extremely rewarding, as many unsold miniature horses, for example feral caught Dartmoors or New Forests, will be destroyed if they can't be sold. That said, some of them would never make good pets at all. This is why you need to have someone by your side with some knowledge.

Most auction animals are from big herds or are feral caught. This means that they could have all manner of health and psychological problems that would not have been picked up on. Feral caught horses at auction also tend to be very young, so if the animal is healthy, you could be getting yourself in for a commitment upwards of 25 years.

### b) Breeders

There are all sorts of arguments in favour of getting your miniature horse from a breeder. Breeders often have lots of advice and will usually offer excellent after care. Local breeders will be able to advise you on things like feed suppliers, veterinary services and farriers. Horses born in captivity are better adjusted to life in captivity. Being able to trace the lineage of a horse will mean you can avoid any congenital diseases.

## 2. *Choosing your miniature horse*

One thing to consider with miniature horses that you might not consider with shorter-lived animals is that you don't necessarily have to get a baby in order to have a long lasting, meaningful relationship with your animal. The fact is that many miniature horses live into their late 20s, and some into their 30s. You need to bare this in mind when thinking about the commitment you are thinking of taking on.

Many miniature horse owners get their first miniature horse at around 6, as they will often have got over their youthful exuberance and will be more settled and calm. It also means a 15 to 20 year commitment, as opposed to a 20-25 year one. Some owners choose only to own much older horses. As miniature horses are generally not for riding anyway, the strength and speed of the animal is not the main attraction. For some, it is important to know and understand the temperament of their new pet before bringing them home to interact with other animals.

If you are getting your miniature horse as a companion to another, older horse, you might want to consider the expected lifespan of your existing horse and trying to match that up, so that when your first animal goes, as heartbreaking and terrible a concept as that is, their miniature companion won't have to face 10 years of lonely pining or end up in the constant cycle of replacing the companion ad infinitum. Older horses, especially ones who have been owned and loved for a longer amount of time by someone else, tend to already have some training.

If you are getting a miniature horse as a first rider for a young child, then an older, calmer animal will often be a better option. Also, if you intend to keep the animal for the rest of it's natural life after being ridden, unless you have a riding school or other, younger, children, you may well end up with a horse no one can use for up to 30 years.

In short, there are many benefits of getting your miniature horse slightly older.

Younger horses, too, have their pros. For one, you will be able to train them to your specifications, and as training can take years, you are better starting training young. If you intend to train your miniature horse for dressage or other similar competitions, training them from younger will often be better than attempting to train them in something completely new at an older age.

Very old miniature horses should only be considered if you have a large veterinary budget and are looking for a slow old thing to potter around your garden or to keep an old nag company. They can be very rewarding animals, even as OAPs, but without a shared history of good times together, very old horses can be a real drain, both financially and emotionally. It is very different caring for a beloved animal that you've loved and cared for for 10 years, and who has loved you back, than caring for one who has only ever been ill and difficult.

# Chapter 14)   Biology

**SKELETON OF A HORSE**

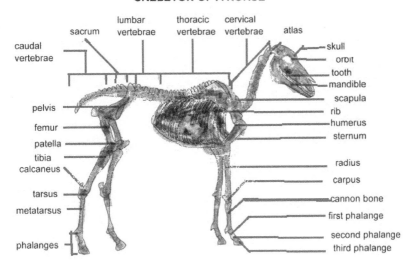

The **horse** (*Equus ferus cabal lus*) is one of two taxonomic subspecies of *Equus ferus*, (the wild horse). It is an odd-toed ungulate –ungulate meaning having hoofs – mammal belonging to the family Equidae. The horse has evolved over the past 45 to 55 million years from a small, multi-toed creature into the large, single-toed animal of today.

A horse's anatomy enables it to make use of speed to escape predators and they have a well-developed sense of balance and a strong fight-or-flight response. Related to this need to flee from predators in the wild is an unusual trait: horses are able to sleep both standing up and lying down. Female horses, called mares, carry their young for approximately 11 months, and a young horse, called a foal, can stand and run shortly following birth.

Most domesticated horses begin training under saddle or in a harness between the ages of two and four. They reach full adult development by age five, and have an average lifespan of between 25 and 30 years.

Horse breeds are loosely divided into three categories based on general temperament: spirited "hot bloods" with speed and endurance; "cold bloods", such as draft horses and some ponies, suitable for slow, heavy work; and "warm bloods", developed from crosses between hot bloods and cold bloods, often focusing on creating breeds for specific riding purposes, particularly in Europe. There are more than 300 breeds of horse in the world today, developed for many different uses.

Depending on breed, management and environment, the modern domestic horse has a life expectancy of 25 to 30 years. Uncommonly, a few animals live into their 40s and, occasionally, beyond.

The following terminology is used to describe horses of various ages:

Foal: a horse of either sex, less than one year old. A nursing foal is sometimes called a *suckling* and a foal that has been weaned is called a *weanling*. Most domesticated foals are weaned at five to seven months of age, although foals can be weaned at four months with no adverse physical effects.

Yearling: a horse of either sex that is between one and two years old.

Colt: a male horse under the age of four. A common terminology error is to call any young horse a "colt", when the term actually only refers to young male horses.

Filly: a female horse under the age of four.

Mare: a female horse four years old and older.

Stallion: a non-castrated, male horse, four years old and older. The term "horse" is sometimes used colloquially to refer specifically to a stallion.

Gelding: a castrated male horse of any age.

Horses have 64 chromosomes. The horse genome was sequenced in 2007. It contains 2.7 billion DNA base pairs, which is larger than the dog genome, but smaller than the human genome or the bovine genome. The map is available to researchers.

Gestation lasts approximately 340 days, with an average range of 320–370 days, and usually results in one foal; twins are rare and will often not both survive. Horses are a periodical species, and foals are capable of standing and running within a short time following birth. Foals are usually born in the spring. The oestrous cycle of a mare occurs roughly every 19–22 days and occurs from early spring into autumn. Most mares enter an *anoestrus* period during the winter and won't come into heat in this period. Foals are generally weaned from their mothers between four and six months of age.

## Breeding

Horses, particularly colts, sometimes are physically capable of reproduction at about 18 months, but domesticated horses are rarely allowed to breed before the age of three, especially females. Horses that are four years old are considered mature, although the skeleton normally continues to develop until the age of six; maturation also depends on the horse's size, breed, sex, and quality of care. Larger horses have larger bones; therefore, not only do the bones take longer to form bone tissue, but also the epiphysis plates are larger and take longer to convert from cartilage to bone. These plates convert after the other parts of the bones, and are crucial to development.

Depending on maturity, breed, and work expected, horses are usually put under saddle and trained to be ridden between the ages of two and four. Although thoroughbred race horses are put on the track as young as the age of two in some countries, horses specifically bred for sports such as dressage are generally not put under saddle until they are three or four years old, because their bones and muscles are not solidly developed. For endurance riding competitions, horses are not deemed mature enough to compete until they are a full 60 calendar months (five years) old.

The critical importance of the feet and legs is summed up by the traditional adage, "no foot, no horse". The horse hoof begins with the distal phalanges, the equivalent of the human fingertip or tip of the toe, surrounded by cartilage and other specialized, blood-rich soft tissues such as the lamiae. The exterior hoof wall and horn of the sole is made of essentially the same material as a human fingernail. The end result is that a horse, weighing on average 500 kilograms (1,100 lb), travels on the same bones as a human would on tiptoe. For the protection of the hoof under certain conditions, some horses have horseshoes placed on their feet by a professional farrier. The hoof continually grows, and in most domesticated horses needs to be trimmed (and horseshoes reset, if used) every five to eight weeks, though the hooves of horses in the wild wear down and re-grow at a rate suitable for their terrain.

**Teeth**

Horses are adapted to grazing. In an adult horse, there are 12 incisors at the front of the mouth, adapted to biting off the grass or other vegetation. There are 24 teeth adapted for chewing, the premolars and molars, at the back of the mouth. Stallions and geldings have four additional teeth just behind the incisors, a type of canine teeth called "tushes". Some horses, both male and female, will also develop one to four very small vestigial teeth in front of the molars, known as "wolf" teeth, which are generally removed because they can interfere with the bite. There is an empty, interdental space between the incisors and the molars where the bite rests directly on the gums, or "bars" of the horse's mouth when the horse is bridled.

An estimate of a horse's age can be made from looking at its teeth. The teeth continue to erupt throughout life and are worn down by grazing. Therefore, the incisors show changes as the horse ages; they develop a distinct wear pattern, changes in tooth shape, and changes in the angle at which the chewing surfaces meet. This allows a very rough estimate of a horse's age, although diet and veterinary care can also affect the rate of tooth wear.

Horses are herbivores with a digestive system adapted to a forage diet of grasses and other plant material, consumed steadily throughout the day. Therefore, compared to humans, they have a relatively small stomach but very long intestines to facilitate a steady flow of nutrients. A 450-kilogram (990 lb) horse will eat 7 to 11 kilograms (15 to 24 lb) of food per day and, under normal use, drink 38 litres (8.4 imp gal; 10 US gal) to 45 litres (9.9 imp gal; 12 US gal) of water. Horses are not ruminants, so they have only one stomach, like humans, but unlike humans, they can digest cellulose, a major component of grass. Cellulose digestion occurs in the cecum, or "water gut", which food goes through before reaching the large intestine. Horses cannot vomit, so digestion problems can quickly cause colic, a leading cause of death.

Horses are prey animals with a strong fight-or-flight response. Their first reaction to threat is to startle and usually flee, although they will stand their ground and defend themselves when flight is impossible or if their young are threatened. They also tend to be curious; when startled, they will often hesitate an instant to ascertain the cause of their fright, and may not always flee from something that they perceive as non-threatening. Most light horse riding breeds were developed for speed, agility, alertness and endurance, which are natural qualities that extend from their wild ancestors. However, through selective breeding, some breeds of horses are quite docile, particularly certain draft horses. Horses are herd animals, with a clear hierarchy of rank led by a dominant individual, usually a mare. They are also social creatures that are able to form companionship attachments to their own species and to other animals, including humans. They communicate in various ways, including vocalizations such as nickering or whinnying, mutual grooming, and body language. Many horses will become difficult to manage if they are isolated, but with training, horses can learn to accept a human as a companion, and thus be comfortable away from other horses. However, when confined with insufficient companionship, exercise, or stimulation, individuals may develop stable vices, an assortment of bad habits, mostly stereotypes of psychological origin, that include wood chewing, wall kicking, "weaving" (rocking back and forth), and other problems.

# Forums and other sources of information

www.miniaturehorsetalk.com

www.horseforum.com

www.lilbeginnings.com

www.forum.horsetopia.com

www.smallesthorse.com

www.horseandhound.co.uk

www.yourhorse.co.uk

www.horsemart.co.uk

www.equine-world.co.uk

www.horsegroomingsupplies.com

# Index